THE MARRIAGE COOK BOOK
By
ADWOBA ADDO-BOATENG

PUBLISHED by PARABLES
Earthly Stories with a Heavenly Meaning

The Marriage Cook Book
Adwoba Addo-Boateng

Published By Parables
February, 2019

All Rights Reserved. No part of this book may be reproduced or utilized in any form or by any means, electronic or mechanical, including photocopying, recording, or by any information storage and retrieval system, without permission in writing from the author.

    ISBN 978-1-945698-94-1
    Printed in the United States of America

Readers should be aware that Internet Web sites offered as citations and/or sources for further information may have been changed or disappeared between the time this was written and the time it is read.

The Marriage Cook Book
By
Adwoba Addo-Boateng

PUBLISHED by PARABLES
Earthly Stories with a Heavenly Meaning

ABOUT THE AUTHOR

Adwoba Addo-Boateng is passionate about teaching the gospel of Christ through practical examples that people can relate to. She strongly believes that we can be the change through Christ. She holds a Bachelor of Arts degree in Psychology and Spanish and a Master of Arts degree in Economic Policy Management from the University of Ghana. She is currently pursuing a PhD in Human and Social Services. She is married with children.

DEDICATION

To my Great grand mum, Nyauga Akissi (Mary Armoo) of blessed memory; a woman who believes that marriage is a God ordained ministry and was a beautiful bride!

ACKNOWLEDGEMENT

All thanks to the Holy Spirit for this inspired book and I am also grateful to Dr. John Dee Jeffries, *Published By Parables,* for his tremendous help in getting my book to readers.

I am forever grateful to everyone who supported my dream in diverse ways.

INTRODUCTION

What could be more exciting and fulfilling than being a beautiful bride in marriage? Everyone could have a blissful marriage, if we exhibit unconditional love to our partners. However, sometimes the things of the world take us away from our divine purpose in the marriage we find ourselves in. Christ's prayer for us is not to take us out of the world but rather he wishes God's protection for us from the evil one. Because, as children of God, we are not of the world, even as he is not of it. He prays for God to sanctify us by the truth; and God's word is truth. As God has sent him into the world, He has also sent us into the world (John 17:15-18). Therefore, as Christians we are not supposed to live according to the world although we may be tempted but the word of God will guide us in our lives. Marriage or relationships are learning processes for us as individuals, so instead of trying to maneuver our marriages by fixing our partners lives to be what we want them to be, let us focus on Christ, so that we can be the person Christ wants us to be. Let us not waste any more time, for time cannot be recovered, grumbling in our hearts what a good partner should be. Rather, being the person that our partner needs is best for our marriages so that we can be used to fulfil God's divine purpose. In addition, there is good in everybody if only we can find it by allowing Christ to open our eyes of understanding and soften our hearts. When we begin to see clearly, we realize that, there is gold underneath the dust. Sometimes, we feel we are in a bad marriage, but then again a "bad marriage" may be an avenue for us to get closer to God by making him our all dependency. Turning all obstacles in our lives into every opportunity to know God is the way to go. Therefore, let us give God a chance in our marriages and he will be with us through it all. Our marriage will no longer be like work, but it will be a journey with Christ.

MARRIAGE IS A JOURNEY WITH CHRIST

Take a back seat, fasten your seatbelt and enjoy the bumpy ride!

When Christ is the driver of your marriage it does not mean that you will not encounter problems. You will definitely fall into potholes, when you fall into those potholes, you will get hurt but since Christ is love, love will drive you out of those potholes. The righteous person may have many troubles, but the lord delivers him from them all (Psalm 34:19). He always redirects our paths if he is driving. On the other hand, when you decide to take the wheel from his hands and drive the marriage yourself, if under any circumstances, you fall into potholes, you would have to drive yourself out of those potholes and you eventually take the front seat and you are in control of your marriage. Since you are not a good driver, you may end up driving yourself into potholes then ditches after ditches, because anything other than love is driving you. Before you realize, you have driven yourself out of the marriage. We should allow Christ to be in the driver's seat by allowing unconditional love to drive us, so that no matter the bumps, ditches and potholes, we know we are safe in his hands and he is in control of our marriages.

COOKING TIPS
TIP #1

BEFORE YOU SAY, I DO

When we want to get married, normally there is a deep psychological need that we want to fulfil. It could be emotional stability, good interpersonal relationship, prestige and self- esteem or financial stability. Accordingly, most of us use the boy- meets-girl -and -finally –get- married approach in life without God. But if we have given our lives to Christ, we need to involve him in all that we do and surrender our lives to him totally. Most of us only involve God when we have a problem, when all is bliss and nice then God is left out of the picture. Marriage is a sacred institution and as such we need to communicate with the Lord in getting a good partner. God is a perfect match maker as he always knows the beginning and the end thus consulting God through prayer for a partner is the initial step to his divine covenant. When Abraham wanted a wife for his son Isaac, he included God in the process (Genesis 24). Being God's servant he did not just get up and choose a wife for his son but he wanted God's own choice for every good and perfect thing is from above, coming down from the father of the heavenly lights who does not change like shifting shadows (James 1:17). Abraham's servant when given the task prayed and asked God to guide him through the process, because he realized that he could not do it alone, he could only do it through God. When we submit totally to God, and recognize the fact that it is only through Christ things can be done, he comes through for us. Abraham's servant wanted a wife for Isaac who was bearing the fruits of the spirit(kindness, humility, politeness) and God showed him a sign that Rebekah was the chosen one (Genesis 24). Houses and wealth are inherited from parents, but a prudent wife is from the Lord (Proverbs 19:14). God always prepares us ahead of the journey if only we allow ourselves in order to be emotionally and mentally ready, equipped with Christ like values and standards. When God chooses a partner for you, you will just know he or she is the one because he or she is God's plan. Not that you won't have problems, there will be problems but God will walk you through it and your partner will support your life long journey, with God being the overseer of the marriage.

TIP #2

GETTING MARRIED TO CHRIST

We all have various reasons why we got married in the first place. Some of us got married for companionship, in order to have children, to boost our self- esteem or to release some sort of financial burden on us as individuals.

Most girls dream of their wedding day with all the glamour, being in their beautiful wedding dresses and getting married to their prince charming. They always imagine friends and family attending this lovely ceremony, spiced with great food, good laughter and cheers. After your ring is worn on that right finger, you feel so satisfied. Of course! This is what you have always wanted. You then wish for a happily ever after. Few years down the line, the prince charming evolves back into a beast, as if the kiss to break that initial spell was anything but a true love kiss. Whilst watching your favorite soap, you appear to be so disinterested, and you gaze at your wedding ring, using your right fingers to turn the ring in different directions. You begin to ask questions; did I make the right decision, why did I not see his character clearly? Is it something I did wrong? Why is my marriage not working? Most people have argued countlessly that marriage is doing more harm than good these days and you feel your marriage is one of those marriages that just will not work. You begin to think of a way out, but before you do, let's look at why God instituted marriage in the first place?

The Genesis of Marriage

Genesis 2:7 "The Lord God formed the man from the dust of the ground and breathed into his nostrils the breath of life; and the man became a living being". After the Lord God made Adam (the first man) an overseer of the Garden of Eden and gave him a helper, a woman called Eve. "The Lord God said it is not good for the man to be alone. I will make a helper suitable for him "(Genesis 2:18). So the man gave names to all the livestock, the birds of the air and all the beast of the field. But for Adam, no suitable helper was found. So the Lord God caused man to fall into a deep sleep; and while he was sleeping, he took one of the man's ribs and closed up the place with flesh. Then the Lord God made a woman from the rib he had taken out of man, and he brought her to the man. The man said, this is now bone of my bones and flesh of my flesh; she shall be called woman for she was taken out of man. For this reason a man will leave his father and mother and be united to his wife, and they will become one flesh. The man and his wife were both naked, and they felt no shame (Genesis 2:20-25). Marriage is an institution designed by God; Marriage is a union with God being the head. God is the only one who has control over the marriage. When we let ourselves go no matter the situation we are facing in a marriage, God comes in and takes over the marriage.

What is the role of husband and wife in marriage?

Wives, submit to your husbands as to the Lord, for the husband is the head of the wife as Christ is the head of the church, his body of which he is the savior. Now as the church submits to Christ, so also wives should submit to their husbands in everything.
Husbands love your wives, just as Christ loved the church and gave himself up for her to make her holy, cleansing her by the washing with water through the word, and to present her to himself as a radiant church, without stain or wrinkle or any other blemish, but holy and blameless (Ephesians 5:22-27).
The role of the husband and wife in Christianity is so clear, the wife should submit and the man should love. Now in modern days, submission on the part of a woman is almost non-existent. In our daily struggles in life, women are faced with more responsibilities, in keeping the home and maintaining a career at the same time. At times, your husband's attitude at home can be so annoying and

unbearable. It gets so worse, especially when you have picked the kids from school and you had a terrible day at work. You are so exhausted, period! Submission may be the last thing on your mind. How then do wives submit in modern times where gender roles are changing over time?

Submission stems out of mutual love and understanding for each other. As a Christian, love should drive you. A Pharisee asked Jesus: Teacher, which is the greatest commandment in the law? Jesus replied: Love the Lord your God with all your heart and with all your soul and with all your mind. This is the first and greatest commandment. And the second is like it: Love your neighbor as yourself (Matthew 22: 36-39). Love is putting other people's needs above yours unconditionally. A Christian lady I met told me, my husband is so disrespectful to me, and how does he expect me to submit. The answer was pretty simple; submission should not be based on what he fails or fails not to do. Submission should be based on God's word and know that as you are submitting to him, you are submitting to Christ. It is a requirement for you as a wife, to place the word of God first in your marriage. Submission and love works hand in hand. As you are submitting to your husband, he in turn will love you so much and you will be heirs together to the grace of life. If a wife submits to her husband and the husband loves the wife, marriage will be a blissful union with no turning back.

Christ's Beautiful Bride

A lady I knew was in a very bad marriage. Her husband disrespected her all the time; her marriage was making her unhappy in life. She was a Christian and her husband was not. She contemplated divorce several times to escape the bad situation in her marriage. As she was thinking about her situation, she thought of a scripture in the bible. Do not be anxious about anything but in everything by prayer and petition, with thanksgiving; present your requests to God. And the peace of God, which transcends all understanding, will guard your hearts and minds in Christ Jesus (Philippians 4:6-7). She turned all her worries and thoughts into prayers. God took control of her marriage. Not that the problems were not there anymore. The problems were there but God was with her all through. No temptation has seized you except what is common to man. And God is faithful; he will not let you be tempted beyond what you can bear. But when you are tempted, he will also provide a way out so that you can bear it (1 Corinthians 10:13). The lady relied on God for all emotional support and made God her all sufficiency and God did the imaginable! The lady realized that she also had some issues which were generating some of the problems in the marriage. Through Christ, she turned over a new leaf. The husband was amazed at how the wife had changed so much and for the better. The more he tried to understand the change, the more confused he was. The wife's life was now shining. She was a testimony and the message of the cross was fully activated in her. Neither do people light a lamp and put it under a bowl. Instead they put it on its stand, and it gives light to everyone in the house. In the same way, let your light shine before others, that they may see your good deeds and glorify your Father in heaven. (Matthew 5:15-16). The icing on the cake was the husband changed his ways too and loved his wife so much. What changed? Christ came into their marriage and Christ was the head. Wives, in the same way submit yourselves to your own husbands so that, if any of them do not believe the word, they may be won over without words by the behavior of their wives, when they see the purity and reverence of your lives (1 Peter 3:1-2). They began to pray together and it was beautiful. For the eyes of the Lord are on the righteous, and his ears are attentive to their prayer, but the face of the Lord is against those who do evil (I Peter 3:12). But at the beginning of creation, God made them male and female. For this reason a man will leave his father and mother and be united to his wife and the two will become one flesh, so that they are no longer two, but one. Therefore what God has put together let no man separate (Matthew 10:6-9).

There is no perfect marriage, for just as your partner is not perfect you are also not perfect. Try to be the change through Christ; *You hypocrite,* first *take the plank* out of your own eye, and then you will see clearly to remove the speck from your brother's eye (Matthew 7:5) for nobody is good except God alone (Matthew 10:18). Be Christ's beautiful bride. Who knows you might win your husband over to Christ. A wife of noble character who can find? She is worth far more than rubies. Her husband has full confidence in her and lacks nothing of value. She brings him good, not harm, all the days of her life (Proverbs 31:10).

Most of the time, we tend to focus too much on the outer appearance, how beautiful we want to look to please our husbands. Of course! There is no harm in trying to do that, for God is a fashionable God, however he does not look at the outward appearance but looks in the heart. "I the LORD search the heart and examine the mind, to reward each person according to their conduct, according to what their deeds deserve" (Jeremiah 17:10). Accordingly, let us try to focus more on the inward man and our relationship with our father, for his holy spirit to dwell in us so that we will live a life through the spirit for his perfect will to be done in our lives.

Charm is deceptive, and beauty is fleeting; but a woman who fears the LORD is to be praised (Proverbs 10:30).

Therefore be imitators of God as dear children. And walk in love, as Christ also has loved us and given himself for us, an offering and a sacrifice to God for a sweet-smelling aroma (Ephesians 5:1-2).

TIP #3

HEALTHY HABITS
DETOX TEA

Take away the flesh

Always take away the things that are toxic from your bodies (sexual immorality, impurity, and debauchery, idolatry and witchcraft: hatred, discord, jealousy, fits of rage, selfish ambition, dissensions, factions and envy, drunkenness, orgies and the like) by living according to the spirit of God . But the fruit of the spirit is love, joy, peace, patience, kindness, goodness, faithfulness; gentleness and self-control (Galatians 5).

AVOID BURN OUT

Grace Exercises

Working too hard on your marriage, will make you experience burn out. Focus on the grace that will see your marriage through not works. And if by grace, then it is no longer by works; if it were, grace would no longer be grace (Romans 11:6).

Tea break

Most times, when you feel like you are the one doing all the work in your relationship, it is about time to have a break and give all the work to God. For the only good worker is God, that makes all of us bad workers and a bad workman quarrels with his tools. In lieu of that, when things are not happening the way it should we blame it on a lot of factors. Let us allow the good workman to work the marriage by entering his rest (Hebrews 4).

TIP #4

MARRIAGE FAVORATTITUDES

Kindness
Patience
Perseverance
Gentle spirit
Humility
Serviceable
Dutiful
Transparency
Openness
Respect
Hope
Faith
Forgiveness

RECIPES FOR SUCCESSFUL MARRIAGES

1. THE PROBLEM: MAN SHALL NOT LIVE BY RICE ALONE

Mr. Allan bought a bag of rice at the supermarket and so happily brought the bag of rice home for his family. Mrs. Allan met her at the doorway and said. Hey, what do we have here? He replied. A bag of rice for the family he replied. Then Mrs. Allan commented, Okay! Mr. Allan repeated, Okay, is that all you will say. What do you want me to say: You have to say thank you. Do you know what I went through to get this bag of rice? Mrs. Allan continued; you bought a bag of rice only for your family and you want me to say thank you, for what? What would you expect me to do if you had taken me to Paris fashion week to shop? Now the situation was getting ugly. It turned into series of fights and arguments.

RECIPE
THANK YOU PIES
Ingredients
½ cup appreciation
¼ cup love
¼ cup humility

METHOD
Humility is one of the key ingredients in marriage, being humble enough to thank your partner for little things will not hurt. If we say we are imitators of Christ, then our attitude should be the same as Christ Jesus who being found in appearance as man, he humbled himself and became obedient to death, even death on a cross (Philippians 2). When we love our partners, we should be able to appreciate them by constantly reminding them that they are appreciated and loved. Giving thanks in all circumstances, for this is the will of God in Christ Jesus (1 Thessalonians 5:18). As you thank your husband for that bag of rice, you are actually thanking

God and being grateful to him for everything, for from him and through him and to him are all things. To him be the glory forever Amen (Romans 11:36).

2. THE PROBLEM: THE CRAVING CALL

Mrs. Grace was a stay at home mom with two kids and was pregnant with a third child. Mrs. Grace has become so picky with her food, a case of pregnancy hormones. She loved one particular type of food in an expensive restaurant. Her husband, being a loving husband always bought it for his wife. It got to a time, the husband was getting fed up because he thought this craving was only going to last for a short time, but it looked as if, the craving was never going to go away. His pocket had become so dry and he wanted ways and means to stop this "luxurious" life without hurting his wife. As usual, Mrs. Grace's call always comes around 1.00 pm to remind her husband of her "luxurious" lunch. This kept on and on, Mrs. Grace really was a time keeper, she never missed an appointment. At exactly 1:00 pm each day, she will make that call. One afternoon, Mrs. Grace called the husband to place the order, when she called; the husband picked up the phone and immediately said, I am not going out to day. Mrs. Grace was so shattered; her husband could not even wait to hear what she had to say.

RECIPE
EASY-PEASY CUP CAKES
Ingredients
½ cup communication
¼ cup love
¼ cup prayer

METHOD
Married life throws us a lot of unexpected reactions from our spouses and we get surprised all the time. Mrs. Grace is pregnant; hey she needs to be doted on by her husband. However, sometimes financial constraints make this doting almost impossible. When there is real love between a couple, communication becomes easier owing to the fact that perfect love drives out fear, because fear has

to do with punishment, the one who fears is not made perfect in love (1 John 4:18). Open and honest communication between husband and the wife is very important in this scenario for the husband to open up on his finances and the wife to understand the situation so that a consensus can be reached as to what decision they should take to satisfy all parties involved. Perhaps, when those cravings come, she can take a prayer walk in the neighborhood to commune with God about her cravings. When we make God, the solver of all our problems, we are able to go through life knowing that he is in control, because his yoke is easy and his burden is light (Matthew 11:30). He can even take those cravings away for peace to reign, nothing is impossible for God.

3. THE PROBLEM: THE SWEETENED MILO DRINK

A couple was struggling to make ends meet; the husband bought a tin of Milo which he assumed will last for a week. After two days, he decided to make a cup of Milo drink and he was so surprised that the tin of Milo he bought two days ago was finished. So he called his wife and said; Honey, how come the tin of Milo is finished? The wife replied sarcastically; yes, it is all finished I have used the whole tin of Milo for breakfast. Then the husband responded, you need to add sugar to the Milo when making the Milo drink so that a tin of Milo can last for a long time. The wife replied, sarcastically again: It is because you do not have money. What is the big deal if I add or do not add sugar to the Milo drink and a tin of Milo gets finished within a day? The husband was infuriated and felt insulted.

RECIPE
ROYAL TREATS
½ cup communication
½ cup respect
½ cup of language full of grace

METHOD
The husband needs to communicate with his wife what the financial situation in the house is, for the wife to understand that they need to cut their coat according to their cloth or manage their resources well. Moreover, a rule of thumb, every man wants to be respected and treated as a king, no matter what the situation is. If you are in Christ and you respect your husband know that you are submitting to Christ. You are doing this in obedience to the word of God. As a Christian, certain words should not come out of your mouth. If anyone considers himself religious and yet does not keep a tight rein on his tongue, he deceives himself and his religion is worthless (James 1:26). Accordingly, your voice should reflect a gentle and quiet spirit, which is worthy in God's sight (1 Peter 3:4).

4. THE PROBLEM: WORDS DON'T DEFINE A PERSON

Gift and Paul were a married couple who lived in Trafalgar square. Gift never showed emotions openly, but she loved Paul to bits. Paul was having issues with Gift's inability to express her love openly. One day, Paul was going to work, when he gave Gift a peck on the cheek and said: I love you, Gift responded Okay. Paul was taken aback at the answer; He wanted Gift to respond with I love you too. He got angry and quickly left the house. After a while, he found solace in another woman who was exactly the type of woman she wanted. The one who could say I love you every minute of the day, give him hugs at the least chance possible. Gradually, their marriage was deteriorating and both Gift and Paul were unhappy.

RECIPE
SCRAMBLE LOVE DO-NOTS
Ingredients
½ cup communication
A dash of love
A pinch of sugar spice

METHOD
Paul and Gift have been socialized differently coming from different backgrounds. Thus, communication is the key so that their differences will be put aside in order for them to work towards a common goal and that is love, through Christ who strengthens them. Moreover, Gift, continued loving her husband in obedience to God irrespective of she and her husband's differences. As Christians, we are supposed to keep the royal law found in the scriptures, love your neighbor as yourself, you are doing right (James 2:8). Paul in turn, reciprocated that love by having a chat with Gift about her inability to express her love openly. Paul found out that Gift had never been loved; accordingly, she was neglected by her parents and sent to a foster home.

Therefore, she just didn't know how to respond to such words. Paul eventually begun loving Gift, the way she was and Gift learned how to respond to Paul, the way he wanted it. My dear brothers, take note of this: Everyone should be quick to listen, slow to speak and slow to become angry, for man's anger does not bring about the righteous life that God desires (James 1:20).

5. THE PROBLEM: THE INCONSIDERATE PARTNER

Mr. and Mrs. Happy lived happily in a two bedroom house. When things took a different turn at work, Mr. Happy had a pay cut owing to management downsizing staff. There was this particular school that Mrs. Happy wanted her ten year old son to attend. Oh My! The school was charging very exorbitant fees which they obviously could not afford even together as a couple. Mr. Happy suggested that they take their son to an equally good school with very low fees comparatively. Mrs. Happy was not happy and rejected the idea. She kept on nagging about the issue; she really wanted to take her son to that school at all cost. This issue was gradually turning into a nightmare.

RECIPE
RECHAUFFE DISH-TRIFLE
Ingredients
½ cup contentment
½ cup management
½ cup prayer
½ cup communication
A pinch of humility

METHOD
Note: A "rechauffe" dish is made using leftover dish to create a new dish.
Pride goes before destruction, a haughty spirit before a fall (Proverbs 16:18). Being content with whatever you have is one value that paves the way for other things that one desires. Paul in the bible learnt to be content whatever the circumstances through Christ who strengthens him. Whatever we want from God, we should ask him through requests, prayers and petition (Philippians 4). If Mrs. Happy really wants that "expensive" school for her son, she should ask God, but note, we cannot set targets for God to meet. But godliness with contentment is great gain, for we brought nothing into the world, and we can take nothing out of it. But if we

have food and clothing, we will be content with that (1 Timothy 6:8). Mr. and Mrs. Happy should have a conversation about the situation and be open about their resources and constraints. Perhaps, Mrs. Happy can take her son to that affordable school and add a home teacher to improve upon the son's academic performance where necessary if it is the will of God.

6. THE PROBLEM: A WORKING WORLD

Honey, will you take out the trash? Mrs. Cooks shouted. I have been working all day and I am really exhausted replied Mr. Cooks. You have been sitting at home all day just taking care of kids, Mr. Cooks added. Do you think it is that easy? I have been working hard taking care of the kids and doing household chores and you say it is nothing, Mrs. Cooks replied. Well, I am sorry but I just can't, I feel it is your work. Mr. Cook concluded.

RECIPE
MINT SYRUP
Ingredients
¼ cup appreciators
½ cup communication
½ cup love

METHOD
Mint is a spice that makes our breath smell nice. It is just not what you say but how you say it. Although Mr. Cooks had a preconceived mind that women's work at home is not really that difficult compared to doing a normal 9-5 office job, he was totally mistaken. Women do more work than men most of the time. A little discretion or appreciation on Mr. Cooks' part would have averted this situation. However, love is gentle and kind. As wives, we need to let our conversation be always full of grace, seasoned with salt, so that we may know how to answer everyone (Colossians 4:6). How would it sound, if Mrs. Cooks acknowledged her husband's work and asked him the help that she wanted? Mrs. Cooks could have gone like this; Sweetheart, I know you are tired and I agree totally but could you please help me with the trash?

7. THE PROBLEM: A DOMESTIC WORLD

Sweetheart, I swept and mopped the floor. I also vacuumed the carpet. What do you think? When I am not around, the house never gets clean. That was Mr. Boast going on and on. Oh! Please! Stop this already. I have been doing this as far as I remember, you just started helping and the whole world should know that you are once in your life helping, Mrs. Boast replied.

RECIPE
HONEY WAFFLES
Ingredients
½ cup communication
½ cup sweet syrup
½ cup peace flour
½ cup appreciators

METHOD
Never kill your partner's initiative even if he does it once in a blue moon, you need to applaud and encourage him or her. Yes, his words might hurt, but we have to forget about that and focus on Christ! After all, he is trying to help! Embrace his help, men generally want to be heard when they are helping, that is okay. It is his way of wanting to be appreciated. Do not descend into the gutters with him, rather be open and love him unconditionally. Let the peace of Christ rule in your hearts, since as members of one body you were called to peace and be thankful (Colossians 3:15).

8. THE PROBLEM: A CHAOTIC DAY

I have had a terrible day at work! I am not ready to listen to your stories about how your day went said Mr. Yell. Mrs. Yell yelled back, yes you have had a terrible day; mine was more terrible than yours.

RECIPE
HEART SHAPED BURGERS
Ingredients
½ cup listening skills
½ cup love
½ cup prayer

METHOD
When we employ great listening skills in a relationship it makes communication great and the marriage very successful. When we are also able to listen without yelling, we are able to understand the other person better. What if, Mrs. Yell had employed reflective listening by understanding how her husband feels and responding appropriately. It wouldn't have resulted in any quarrel. But now we must rid ourselves of all such things as these: anger, rage, malice, slander, and filthy language from our lips (Colossians 3:8). When we are married, sometimes, we have to let ourselves go and put our partner's needs before us. As we are seeking our partner's needs, God will also seek our needs. Love is not rude, it is not self-seeking, it is not easily angered and it keeps no record of wrongs (1 Corinthians 13:5). In addition, prayer is also very important in a relationship. Mrs. Yell should pray for Christ to come into the husband's heart to take the anger away.

9. THE PROBLEM: THE RICHER WIFE

Mrs. Rich was a very wealthy woman who owned many businesses and estates. She fell in love with a man from a modest family; they lived happily never after. Mrs. Rich was rich and so proud. She called the shots due to the fact that she had the money. Mr. Rich on the other hand, had everything he ever wanted, but not happiness.

RECIPE
LEAN MEAT SOUP
Ingredients:
¼ cup spirit filled water
¼ cup love
¼ cup humility
¼ cup submission

METHOD
Love is no respecter of persons, when we love someone; we have to love that person with all our being. You knew who he was and you promised to love him, no matter what. Love also does not degrade anyone rather love is inclusion and acceptance. When you see yourself as being married to Christ, would you mistreat Christ? When we tend to live according to the spirit, we realize that things of the flesh amount to nothing. And we bear the fruits of the spirit which is love, joy, peace, patience, kindness, goodness, gentleness and self-control. Against such things there is no law (Galatians 5:22).

10. THE PROBLEM: ACADEMIC POMPOSITY

Mr. Edu was a high school leaver, who married a master's degree graduate. Mr. Edu worked in a paint store whilst Mrs. Edu worked in a high profile law firm. Mr. Edu decided to take care of the kids, since he had more time on his hands than his wife. They did this for a couple of years, until Mr. Edu decided to further his education by enrolling in a university for his bachelor's degree. Mrs. Edu angrily rejected to it and these were her words: If you further your education, who will take care of the kids? I have no time.

RECIPE
PINEAPPLE UPSIDE DOWN
Ingredients
½ cup kindness
½ cup love
½ cup negotiation skills
½ cup communication

METHOD
The entire law is summed up in a single command: Love your neighbor as yourself, if you keep on biting and devouring each other, watch out or you will be destroyed by each other (Galatians 5:14-15). The tables are turned now, it is better to be kind than to be right for love is kind. He wants to develop himself, what is the big deal? Mrs. Edu should rather be supportive and negotiate the best way to take care of the kids taking into consideration that everyone has a dream to fulfil. The fact that you are married does not mean that you should throw your dreams away. You can have a successful career and a great family life if love is the key ingredient in your marriage.

11. THE PROBLEM: THE OLDER WOMAN

Mrs. Oldie was two years older than her husband. To Mr. Oldie it felt like she was ten years older than he was, owing to the fact that she made unitary decisions at home; Mr. Oldie was beginning to feel uncomfortable. One day, Mrs. Oldie rented a house without the knowledge of Mr. Oldie. Mr. Oldie has had it; that was the last straw that broke the camel's back. He did not want the marriage anymore.

RECIPE
PANCAKE WITH HUMBLE SYRUP
1 ounce communication
2 ounces self- control
3 ounces of knowledge
1 gallon of humble syrup

METHOD
The fact that you are older than your husband does not mean you are in control, you should be humble. Men, in general, want to be in control. We should all aim at an egalitarian relationship, where couples disagree to agree to make a decision in order for peace to reign." But he gives us more grace. That is why scripture says: God opposes the proud but gives grace to the humble (James 4:6).

12. THE PROBLEM: THE UNSYMPATHETIC MAN

Mrs. Pots has been taking the kids to school, ever since they got married. One day, Mrs. Pots fell ill, so he complained to Mr. Pots. She said, Mr. Pots I am not feeling well today. Mr. Pots looked at her in a very unconcerned way, so who will take the kids to school, he added. Mrs. Pots replied, you are very insensitive and unfeeling. When Mrs. Pots got well she was no more interested in the marriage.

RECIPE
PAWPAW FOOL
Ingredients
2 ounce of Prayer
2 ounces of letting go
2 ounces of forgiveness

METHOD
Jesus is the good shepherd and the good shepherd lays down his life for the sheep (John 10:11). If Jesus laid down his whole life for us, why can't he take care of us if we let him in our situation by abiding in him? Obviously, Mr. Pots is being insensitive and unfeeling for reasons we do not know so we cannot judge. However, do not be quickly provoked in your spirit, for anger resides in the laps of fools (Ecclesiastes 7: 9). Christ is love and love is forgiveness, to be a Christian and live according to his word, we must be fools for Christ sake. For the message of the cross is foolishness to those who are perishing, but to us who are being saved it is the power of God. For it is written: "I will destroy the wisdom of the wise; the intelligence of the intelligent I will frustrate" (1 Corinthians 1:18-19).

13. THE PROBLEM: THE GRUMBLING WIFE

Mrs. Grumbly complains about everything in life. Her mother-in law was about to visit and she hated the idea. Sweetheart she affectionately called her husband anytime she wanted a favor. I don't think your mother should come now; our house is too small to accommodate another person. What are you saying replied Mr. Grumbly, but the guest room is vacant? Errr, Mrs. Grumbly stammered, I have my stuff in there and I do not want anyone occupying that room. Mr. grumbly got angry and said sometimes, I really do not know you!

RECIPE
ENDURING PUMPKIN PIE
1 ounce of the word of God
1 ounce of prayer
I ounce of tolerance
1 ounce of love
Enduring essence

METHOD
Don't grumble against each other, brothers or you will be judged. The judge is standing at your door! (James 4:9). Dwelling on the word of God should be every person's focus in life. When we live according to the word of God it shapes our lives. When we become hospitable to people both around us and afar, we are doing the will of God. Above all love each other deeply, because love covers over a multitude of sins. Offer hospitality to one another without grumbling (1 Peter 4:8-9).

14. THE PROBLEM: THE IMPATIENT WIFE

Mrs. Hurry wanted a car so badly even though she could not afford it, neither could her husband. She was coercing her husband to get her a car, her husband was choking with her incessant demands of getting her a car. She finally managed to secure a car loan to buy a car herself. Since she did not know anything about cars, she bought a car with a very bad engine. Few months later, the car broke down and she had to resell the car at a very cheap price. She incurred huge losses and was left with no car at all.

RECIPE
CHOCOLATE COOKIES WITH PATIENT CHIPPINGS
Ingredients
2 ounces word of God
2 Ounces Prayer
A sprinkle of Patient chippings

METHOD
When we turn all our needs to God, through prayer and wait for his timely intervention we have the peace that cannot be understood by human minds. God always answers prayers according to his will and in his time therefore we have to wait. So, Mrs. Hurry should be joyful in hope, patient in affliction, and faithful in prayer (Romans 12:12). She should also allow God to handle the situation instead of handling it herself. Again, she should also humble herself under God's mighty hand, casting all her anxieties unto the Lord, for the Lord to lift her up in due time (1 Peter 5).

15. THE PROBLEM: THE VERBALLY ABUSIVE WIFE

Mrs. Shout ran down the stairs holding her lab coat in her hands. She was very late to work at the hospital. Her husband said, honey could you please book an appointment for me at the dentist during lunchtime. Are you kidding? You just sit down and you want everything to be done for you. Get up and do something for yourself.

RECIPE
TAMING BARBECUE SAUCE
1 cup of word of God
1 cup of prayer
A Pinch of taming spice

METHOD
We should always try to tame our tongues in any relationship we find ourselves in. When we let Christ into our hearts, he tames our tongues. A gentle answer turns away wrath, but a harsh word stirs up anger (Proverbs15:1). When we talk sweetly to others even though we many not want to do the task, it puts the other person at ease and peace reigns. In addition, the tongue also is a fire, a world of evil amongst the parts of the body. It corrupts the whole person, sets the whole course of his life on fire, and is itself set on fire by hell (James 3:8).

16. THE PROBLEM: DISHONESTY IS LOSS

Mrs. Hon was married to a man who never spent his money on anything luxurious. He bought a new car which was always parked in front of their estate where they lived because he felt it was very expensive driving the car to and from work every day. So he joined the company's bus every morning to get to work. Although the company's bus arrives a bit earlier, therefore, he had to get up very early in the morning; he felt it was a better bargain. Mrs. Hon on the other hand, wanted to drive her husband's treasured car to work but thought he was going to say no. So she sneaked every morning and drove the car to work every day whilst her husband was away. She always watched the fuel gauge and packed the car just as it was. This went on for some time and she was never caught. Until one day she drove the car as usual and met her husband who was returning home from work because he was not feeling too well. Mr. Hon was disappointed in Mrs. Hon and decided he did not want the marriage anymore.

RECIPE
TRUTHFUL FRIED RIPED PLANTAIN WITH HONEST BEANS STEW
Ingredients
1 ounce of truth
1 ounce of word of God
2 ounces of honesty

METHOD
Honesty is always the best policy. Being open and truthful at all times irrespective of how you feel the other person may react is definitely always the way to go to live a godly life. When the word of God dwells in you, the spirit of God lives in us and we worship God in spirit and in truth. We do away with all kinds of evil and our inner man is strengthened day by day so that we can get closer to God for his grace to be activated in our lives. In contrast, when you belong to your father, the devil, you want to carry out your father's desires by not holding to the truth (John 8:44). If we

say God is our father in heaven, we should be truthful at all times, for grace and truth comes from Jesus Christ (John 1:17).

17. THE PROBLEM: THE ANGRY WIFE

Mrs. B walked from the grocery store back home with lots of shopping bags full of groceries. Her husband saw her coming and quickly slammed the door. Mrs. B was so angry and she managed to open the door herself, left the shopping bags on the kitchen floor and went to a neighbor's house. That day, there was no dinner in the B's house. The next day, Mrs. B was still angry and refused to talk to her husband for weeks.

RECIPE
BANANA FORGIVERS
Ingredients
1 ounce communication
½ cup forgivers
½ cup love

METHOD
If Mrs. B had communicated with her husband she will know why he slammed the door, sometimes what you think is not what it is. Mrs. B should forgive her husband, just as Christ forgave us our sins. We all have blemishes, but forgiveness is love. It is okay to get angry but in your anger do not sin. Do not let the sun go down while you are still angry, and do not give the devil a foothold (Ephesians 4:26-27).

18. THE PROBLEM: WHEN SEX IS A CHORE

Mrs. S was so tired on Saturday night. She sat on the kitchen stool recounting the work she has done that day. Oh boy! It had been a terrible day taking care of the kids and doing the household chores whilst Mr. S sat in the hall watching TV. At bedtime, Mr. S touched his wife's dress in a very seductive way. Mrs. S screamed, look here, I am so tired don't you get it!

RECIPE
COUPLE SWEET CANDIES
Ingredients
1 cup communication
1 cup unconditional love
1 cup submission

METHOD
Love is sweet and not bitter. Okay, let's get candid here; it is annoying to watch your husband relax in the hall whilst you get busy in the house trying to fix everything. You feel he has not been an equal partner in taking care of the home, which is true. We could also conclude that Mrs. S secretly despises the husband; however, she needs to have that conversation with her husband about helping her at home. Mrs. S could also ask her husband for the needed help, there is actually nothing to lose if we ask. The worst thing to happen is Mr. S will say no. Mrs. S should also pray about it to God for his will to be done in such a situation. Moreover, the word of God says that, now as the church submits to Christ, so also wives submit to their husbands in everything (Ephesians 5:24), not submission on certain things but in everything. The Apostle Paul concludes this by saying that a wife's body does not belong to her alone but also to her husband. Therefore submit it all to Christ (1 Corinthians 7:4). Through Christ, Mrs. S will be able to accept and love her husband fully even with his flaws.

19. THE PROBLEM: THE GIRLFRIEND IS HYPE

As Mr. and Mrs. Boring strolled down the street, to get to the shopping center, they were both feeling so awkward. They had not gone out together as a couple in years. Their lives had become so monotonous juggling career and children. They hardly had time for each other therefore their relationship was tearing apart. As they were about crossing the main road, Mr. Boring took the lead and crossed the road leaving the wife behind. Mrs. Boring had difficulty in crossing the road because she has been a victim of a car accident and was therefore scared. Mrs. Boring thought of the past, when they were not married, how Mr. Boring had always held her hand to cross roads. Why has he changed over the years? He doesn't care anymore, she said to herself.

RECIPE
DATE SOUP
Ingredients
1 ounce of love
1 ounce of communication
A pack of dates

METHOD
It is the history together with your partner that makes the person special and unique. Mrs. Boring should ask herself what she was doing in the past that she is not doing anymore. Perhaps Mr. Boring is also reacting to the way he is being treated. Marriage should be long term dating. When people marry, they quickly settle into the husband and wife roles and when kids come in, it gets worse, there is actually no couple time. In busy schedules, couples should make time for themselves. Even if the couple has tight schedules, they should go for a date at home when the kids are asleep.

20. THE PROBLEM: THE CHEATING WIFE

Mrs. Cheatskate's husband is an army officer who is on a peace keeping mission in another country for two years. Mrs. Cheatskate got herself a boyfriend to warm her bed since her husband is never there.

RECIPE
MORAL RICE PUDDING
Ingredients
1 cup of Prayer
1 cup of the word of God

METHOD
When we dwell on the word of God and we pray often, the will of God is done in our lives. When we are saturated with the word of God, it becomes difficult to live according to the flesh. Mrs. Cheatskate has a need, but it is better to pray to God to allow God to fulfil that need instead of fulfilling that need herself. Food for the stomach and the stomach for food- but God will destroy them both. The body is not meant for sexual immorality, but for the Lord, and the Lord for the body (1 Corinthians 7:13).

21. THE PROBLEM: HE IS NOT IN THE BIRTHDAY CLUB

Can you believe that my husband forgot my birthday? Gladys said to Grace. Like seriously? What kind of husband does that? How on earth could he forget? I think he is seeing someone else, Grace added.

RECIPE
ABIDING CLUB SANDWICH
Ingredients
1 ounce communication
1 ounce of love
1 ounce of abiding in Christ flour
A dash of forgiveness

METHOD
In our busy schedules sometimes you can forget your own birthday, so it is actually no big deal to remind your husband in the morning if you feel he has forgotten your birthday. Furthermore, when you abide in Christ, He becomes your friend. If you remain in me and my words remain in you, ask whatever you wish; and it will be given to you (John 15:7). You can tell God it is your birthday and the Holy Spirit will remind your husband about your birthday and when the Holy Spirit does it, it is so beautiful.

22. THE PROBLEM: THE PICKY HUSBAND

Jane prepared her husband's favorite dish and hurriedly dashed down the hall, beaming with smiles, she said, Honey I made your favorite dish? Peter her husband replied; Oh! I am sorry Jane; I don't feel like eating that food today? Can you cook something else? Jane's beaming smile turned into a big frown.

RECIPE
APPLE PICKLE SAUCE
Ingredients
1 cup of Love
1 cup of Christ
1 cup of Tolerance
1 cup of Patience

METHOD
Sometimes we want to pull a surprise for our loved ones and we end up getting surprised. Whatever the case may be we should be completely humble and gentle, be patient, bearing with one another in love (Ephesians 4:2) just as Christ taught us.

23. THE PROBLEM: THE NOT TOO TRENDY HUSBAND

As Mrs. Style was walking down the hallway, she was wondering whether her red pencil skirt matched her green flowery blouse. As such she didn't notice her husband coming, so she bumped into him. Oh my! Not again, are you wearing those baggy jeans in a skinny jeans world? I am not going to the party with you dressed like this.

RECIPE
STYLISH BUTTER-FLIES
Ingredients
16 ounces of Love
10 ounces of prayer
A tablespoon of sugar toppings

METHOD
When we marry, we need to keep up with fashionable trends so that we may look attractive to each other. Attraction is always the first thing that brings people together as couples. Why lose that attraction, if you are now married? What Mrs. Style can do is to volunteer to go for clothes shopping with her husband so that she can pick up trendy clothes that she will like him to wear. With prayer as well, the husband will come along, never underestimate the power of prayer it always does the unimaginable. Complement him when he wears those clothes and he will feel loved and always have the butter- fly feeling when he is on the same page with his wife.

24. THE PROBLEM: COLOGNE IS NOT IN HIS SHOPPING LIST

Ama's husband walked into the room and said Ama, how do I look? Ama turned around; her husband looked great but he was wearing her perfume? I have told you time and time again, I do not like you wearing my perfume? I don't even know why you cannot buy your own perfume? Ama replied and angrily turned away. Her husband was so disappointed and ashamed that Ama didn't say anything about what he was wearing but rather dwelt on the perfume he used.

RECIPE
KINDERS DE PARFUM
Ingredients
20 ounces of kinders
10 ounces letting go chilies
1 gallon of appreciating syrup

METHOD
Let's face it; it can be very annoying when your husband walks into the room wearing your perfume. Most wives hate that, but we should always let ourselves go as Christians and be kind to others, because love does not dishonor others, it is not self-seeking, it is not easily angered, it keeps no record of wrongs. (1 Corinthians 13:5). Don't focus on the negatives, but focus on the positives. Sometimes, it is better you overlook it and be nice; you have nothing to lose if you do.

25. THE PROBLEM: HEY! I CHANGED MY HAIRSTYLE

Sika walked in from the salon very exhausted, she had spent the whole day in the salon fixing her hair. At least it was worth the hassle, her hair was looking nice and smelling sweet. She wanted her husband to complement her hairstyle, so she kept on turning her hair in front of her husband but the husband never noticed her hairstyle.

RECIPE
FOCUS CHRIST FLAVORED ICE CREAM
Ingredients
16 ounces Christ
16 ounces Prayer
A pinch of forget me spice

METHOD
Let Christ be the center of your marriage always. If he doesn't see it, Christ does. We should always seek favor and approval from God and not man, although, it would have been nice for him to notice and complement his wife's hair style. The Apostle Paul said in Galatians 1:10 that it is God's approval that we need in order to be bondservants of Christ. When we tend to shift focus from God to men we tend to dwindle the relationship between us and our heavenly father and in conclusion we worry about everything we should not bother ourselves with.

26. THE PROBLEM: A DISORGANISED ROOM

Queen shouted on top of her voice, Chris where are you? I just laid the bed and you sat on it right now and you have ruined everything. Chris responded, but I didn't do anything to the bed, I just sat on it. Queen continued, I am wondering how you sit on beds, obviously you really have a problem.

RECIPE
WHOLESOME LOVEBREAD WITH HAUSA KOKO
Ingredients
A pint of loving wholly
2 ounces of embracing juice

METHOD
When you love someone, you love with your whole heart and that should be practical here. You take the good with the bad, if there is something you can supplement with you do it. He or she may learn from you and begin to do things just the way you want it, if you approach the whole situation with love. For a wife is a man's suitable helper. The Lord God said, "It is not good for the man to be alone. I will make a suitable helper for him" (Genesis 2:18).

27. THE PROBLEM: WHEN THE FLUSH DOES NOT WORK

Afia entered the bathroom to ease her bowels. She was irritated to find out that her husband had used the place and left without flushing. Hey Johnny, why do you still do this? I can't be cleaning up after you. You create the mess and you expect me to clean it up.

RECIPE
CLEAN SYSTEM BROWNIES
Ingredients
A cup of water
Letting go flavoring

METHOD
Telling your husband politely about how difficult it is for you to put up with his attitude is the first step. However, Christ always cleans up our mess, even when we don't deserve it, no matter how dirty we are. He died a shameful death to take away our sins by nailing it on the cross, so why can't we clean other people's mess when we can. When we tend to live according to the spirit, things like this will not cause any problem. Yes, you can be irritated but you will be quickly reminded by the Holy Spirit that the greatest among you will be your servant. For whoever exalts himself will be humbled, and whoever humbles himself will be exalted (Matthew 23:11-12).

28. THE PROBLEM: THE NOT TOO GOOD SHEPHERD

Ama relied on her husband for everything. The husband was getting choked about the situation; Ama's over-reliance on her husband was becoming too stressful for him to handle. One day, Ama told her husband, hubby could you get that pink dress for me? Her husband was now tired, it was getting overbearing for him. He told Ama bluntly, I am tired of you using me all the time, get up and do something for yourself. Ama was devastated.

RECIPE
SHEPHERD'S PIE
10 ounces of Christ
10 ounces of abiding Love
A scoop of openness cream

METHOD
God is the only true love you can ever find. He is the good shepherd and the good shepherd, takes care of his sheep all the time. Christ should be our all dependency in our lives. When we make Christ our all in all, by abiding in him, we stand on that solid rock and all other grounds become sinking sand. Christ becomes the only thing you hold on to, and you take all your nutrients from the vine to sustain you. And my God will meet all your needs according to the riches of his glory in Christ Jesus (Philippians 4:19).

29. THE PROBLEM: WHOSE CHILD IS IT?

Amy felt that her daughter should follow her footsteps and do ballet at school. Her husband on the contrary also felt that his daughter should do karate since he is a karate teacher. They were both confusing the child based on whose footsteps to follow. During one of their arguments Amy snapped back and said she is my child; allow her to follow her mum. Her husband responded she is also my child, let me decide. That was the beginning of an unhappy marriage.

RECIPE
GET AWAY SCONES
Ingredients
2 cups of Christ
2 cups of love

METHOD
The child belongs to God. We are just custodians of children to train them up in the way of God to live fulfilling lives. When we allow God to have his way with his child that he has placed in our care, the child makes choices that God wants them to make and they are not influenced by their dad or mum's profession, career or hobby. Our job on earth is to guide them through the work that God has already given them. And yet his work has been finished since the creation of the world (Hebrews 4).

30. THE PROBLEM: THE MOBILE PHONE SAGA

Aba has always been wondering, why her husband always take the phone to the bathroom anytime he receives certain calls. She was so curious; she wanted to find out the reason for that attitude. Her husband mistakenly left the phone on the couch in the hall whilst picking something from the bedroom one afternoon. Aba hurriedly sneaked and picked up the phone, she quickly scrolled through the messages. As luck would have it all, her husband dashed in and she was caught red handed with the phone.

RECIPE
TEA WITH TRUST ICE
Ingredients
1 cup of trust ice
1 cup of love
1 cup of trust
1 cup of prayer

METHOD
Partners should not pry; everybody wants that moment where he or she does not want to share certain information. Respect that! But be open to your partner whenever he wants to share any information with you. When you are married to someone, you may have doubts about certain behavior he puts up. However, trusting in the one who gave you the marriage will see your marriage to the end. Like I always say, God is the head of every relationship; things might not be exactly how we want it to be. But when we pray about our fears to God and wait for his timely intervention, we lean not on our own understanding (Proverbs 3:5) which normally worsens the situation.

31. THE PROBLEM: THE INTERRACIAL MARRIAGE

Coming from different backgrounds or better still different continents, Ava and Mike were married in a lavish ceremony. After the people were gone, they had to really marry two lives together, it was tough. The different cultures were becoming a stumbling block to the extent that the marriage was breaking down gradually.

RECIPE
MIXED VEGETABLE SOUP
Ingredients
2 cups of love
1 cup of understanding

METHOD
Love is when you are able to live together with people from different backgrounds. It doesn't mean that you will not have differences, you will surely have. However when we make God the center of our marriages, he guides us through the differences and we are able to live at peace with each other and understand each other better. When you are in Christ, there is neither Jew or Greek, slave nor free, male or female, for you are all one in Christ Jesus (Galatians 3:28).

32. THE PROBLEM: THE BETRAYAL

Nana and Ewura have been in a blissful marriage for fifteen years. Their marriage was a model for other Christians in their community to follow. Nana met a very attractive girl in the church choir and they were immediately an item. Ewura got to know and confronted Nana. He confessed to his wife that yes, he had indeed cheated on her and asked for forgiveness. Ewura didn't want to forgive her husband.

RECIPE
FORGIVERS KHEBAB
Ingredients
1 ounce of forgivers
1 ounce of love

METHOD
Our partners disappoint us all the time and we get so hurt, but do we know how many times we have disappointed God and he always forgives us. So therefore, just as Christ forgave our sins, we must also try and forgive the sins of others. It works hand in hand. Forgive us our sins, as we also forgive everyone who sins against us, and lead us not into temptation (Luke 11:4). If we are not able to forgive then we do not love. Love is self-emptying and you cannot self-empty yourself if you do not forgive. If it is possible, as far as it depends on you, live at peace with everyone (Romans 12:18).

33. THE PROBLEM: THE BATHROOM CHALLENGE

Mr. and Mrs. Perfect have been married for just three months and they want to call it quits. The reason is simple and complicated at the same time. Mr. Perfect squeezes toothpaste from the middle to the disgust of Mrs. Perfect who squeezes toothpaste from the tail end of the tube.

RECIPE
REST FISH
Ingredients
10 cups of love
10 cups of Christ

METHOD
It is amazing how trivial things like toothpaste can make partners separate. I always say, when faced with situations like this, ponder over this question, why did I get married? If the reason why you got married in the first place is to love your partner till death do you part. So why then is a toothpaste doing you part? We promised to love our partners with all their baggage. Accept one another, then just as Christ accepted you, in order to bring praise to God (Romans 15:7).

34. THE PROBLEM: A COLD NIGHT

Anna's husband enjoys keeping late nights. One day, he went out and as usual he came back very late. Anna was not asleep; she heard the sound of her husband's engine but didn't budge. Her husband parked his car and alighted from the car, slammed the door and walked straight to their house. He peaked through the window to see whether the lights were on and he was glad they were. He rang the doorbell severally and Anna never answered deliberately. He was so angry and worst of all he had to sleep in his car the whole night.

RECIPE
SPAGHETTI WITH SHREDDED PATIENT SAUCE
Ingredients
10 ounces shredded love Vegetable
10 ounces of Patience

METHOD
When we are in love, we have to be patient with our partners accommodating his or her flaws. When couples want to change each other's behavior, then the conflicts start emerging. Please remember that you cannot change anyone's behavior, only God can. Pray about your partner's behavior to God and let patience have its perfect work, so that you may be perfect and complete, lacking nothing (James1:4).

35. THE PROBLEM: KARATE TRAINING

Sue was constantly arguing and quarreling with her husband over very trivial things. There was not even a single day without a squabble or misunderstanding. Her husband was getting fed up and he was contemplating ending the marriage.

RECIPE
FIGHT RIGHT CRUSHES
Ingredients
10 ounces of Christ
10 ounces of love

METHOD
Add Christ and Love to form a perfect mixture. Love is not rude, it is not self- seeking, it is not easily angered, and it keeps no record of wrongs (1 Corinthians 13:5). When we love we overlook each other's mistakes and focus on the positives whilst we allow God to strengthen the negatives. The Apostle Paul said when we are weak, then Christ's power rests on us so that we become strong (2 Corinthians 12: 9). So therefore put on the fighting belt of righteousness and put God first in all you do.

36. THE PROBLEM: BOXING RING

Ashley and Joe were constantly competing against each other. Joe wanted to further his education, Ashley thought she was being left behind and also followed suit. Ashley changed jobs and Joe also changed his job even though his former job was greater than the latter. They always wanted to outperform the other. This went on for some time, now the healthy competition has turned out to be unhealthy to the extent that it was beginning to affect their marriage.

RECIPE
GOLDEN RINGS SHAWARMA
Ingredients
10 spoonful of Encouragement
10 spoonful of timing

METHOD
There is no competition in marriage; rather couples are expected to complement each other. Partners should encourage each other in areas where one may be deficient in. However, it is okay to have healthy competition in marriage to encourage each other to aspire higher. But when the competition turns unhealthy, the focus of the marriage shifts from lovers to competitors which ultimately destroy the marriage in the long run.

37. THE PROBLEM: THE CRITIC

Jones has been helping Mary to clean the house. It was his day off from work and he decided to help with the household chores. They had shared the work; Mary was cooking whilst Jones was vacuuming the carpet. Mary set the lunch on the table at the far corner of their hall after each finished their share of the work. Jones came into the hall refreshed after having a bath, he sat down and begun to eat. A few minutes after they begun eating, Mary noticed that her favorite vase she bought from the Chinese antique shop had fallen off the shelf and cracked whilst Jones was cleaning. She got angry and accused Jones of not being too careful whilst cleaning.

RECIPE
GRATEFUL GRAPES
Ingredients
1 cup of appreciation
A pack of grateful grapes

METHOD
We should always look out for the good in every partner and praise him or her instead of blaming or judging him or her. Do not judge, or you too will be judged, for in the same way you judge others, you will be judged and with the measure you use, it will be measured to you (Matthew 7:2). Mr. Jones did no harm by helping unfortunately a vase was cracked in the process. Praising a partner when expected elicits more positive behavior from that person. Even if you should criticize do it appropriately, by appreciating his effort and constructively turning a negative outcome into a positive outcome.

38. THE PROBLEM: THE ROOMMATES

Sophie and Simon have been married for five years; their marriage has turned sour owing to very busy careers. They hardly have time for each other. They exchange normal pleasantries in the morning and they came back late at night often very tired. They frequent fast food joints and their dining table has been turned into a desk top library with dusty books. The couple is nothing more than roommates.

RECIPE
BONDING CREAMED POTATOES
Ingredients
1 tube of bonding cream
10 ounces of love

METHOD
Marriage is for companionship, once you decide to marry, you promised to be there for each other. So why has the job taken center stage in your lives? It is good to work, yes! But let's also prioritize our marriage by having quality time for each other so that we can know each other better for a stronger bond. If you claim you love your partner, you will make time for each other.

39. THE PROBLEM: BLAME GAMES

Julie is always blaming Stan for marrying her into a wretched and miserable life. Stan was a construction worker who worked on building projects, but until recently he was not able to cater for his family anymore because the building projects were not coming as they used to.

RECIPE
FAITH PUDDING
Ingredients
4 ounces of love
4 ounces of faith
4 ounces of longsuffering

METHOD
Love is accepting someone in totality and love finds no fault with each other, accordingly long suffering is one of the attributes of love. Julie's faith should be in God to turn the situation around instead of blaming Stan for this situation. Julie should turn all her frustration into prayers and also treating Stan right so that her prayers will be answered, the prayer of the righteous is powerful and effective (James 5:16).

40. THE PROBLEM: LOVE BREWED IN A RICH POT

Sylvia has been married to Timothy for six years. Sylvia was a fashionista; she always spends her money on high end fashion. Down the line, Timothy could not fund this lifestyle because there were other more important things to take care off. Sylvia grew out of love for Timothy because Timothy could not meet her demands. She supposedly fell in love with Cyril, a banker, although she was married because he was wealthy. Cyril's parents were self- made billionaires who owed a chain of stores in the big city.

RECIPE
SIMPLE FRUIT SALAD
Ingredients
8 ounces of Christ
8 ounces of decency
8 ounces of contentment
8 ounces of commitment

METHOD
When we are in Christ, we cannot serve God and money; Christ should drive you not money. For the love of money is the root of all kinds of evil. Some people eager for money, have wandered from the faith and pierced themselves with many griefs (1 Timothy 6:10). Marriage is a holy commitment between two people instituted by God. As such we should be content in whatever circumstances. When you are content with the little that you have, you will be happy in a relationship no matter what. But when there is discontentment, desires set in then after desire has conceived, it gives birth to sin, when it is full grown gives birth to death (James 1:15).

41. THE PROBLEM: THE MISTAKE

Jane was juggling the responsibility of raising five kids and a career in a marketing industry. Everyone thought Jane was doing an incredible job and was always referred to as a super woman except her husband. Her husband Jack was always criticizing Jane for focusing more on her career than her children. Jane also thought she was doing her best in the circumstances she found herself in. One day, Jane really had long hours at work so she called the day care to inform them she will be late in picking the kids. Jane had some deadlines to meet and there was no way out since Jack normally works longer hours than Jane. About 7 pm she picked the kids up and drove home. When she got home, she was so exhausted; she put the kids to sleep and slept herself forgetting to lock the doors. A burglar crept in and took Jack's laptop away. When Jack came back he realized the door was not locked and wondered what was going on. He entered and found the house completely disorganized. He checked in the kids' room where the kids were soundly asleep, he checked on Jane she was asleep too. That was when it dawned on Jack that there has been an incident of burglary. He checked the hall and realized that his laptop was stolen. Then he yelled, Jane! Jane! Jane was still sleepy but managed to get up and realized that they had been robbed. The only thing missing was Jack's laptop, she felt very sorry for not locking the door. Jack was so furious and shouted you have destroyed my life; you are such an irresponsible woman.

RECIPE
SAFE GINGERBREAD HOUSE
Ingredients
5 ounces of love
5 ounces of letting go
5 ounces of prayer
A pinch of appreciation & recognition salt

METHOD
Always do things in your marriage as if you are working for the Lord; Marriage is the Lord's work. It is obvious that Jack has a problem; hence we should always pray for the lord's people for we are all intercessors. Jane should bear in mind that she can never change Jack, but she can be the change through Christ for God to take over the marriage. Even if your husband does not appreciate you bear in mind that God really does and he sees it all. It is a bit disheartening to go through all this in a day and your husband adding to the situation by becoming so insensitive and putting all the blame on you for a so called irresponsible act. There is a better and bigger love up there, just embrace yourself in that love and have a big heart of forgiveness. The word of God will be your guide and your strength.

42. THE PROBLEM: SUCCESS DOES NOT COME WITH KIDS

Angela had a thriving career in a business management firm when she got married. After some time, when the kids started coming in it was tough concentrating on the kids and the career at the same time. So Angela decided to stay at home for a while to take care of the kids whilst they relied on her husband Fiifi's salary for their upkeep. This plan went on smoothly and everyone was happy until Fiifi started complaining about every little thing. He thought he was doing all the hard work whilst Angela and the kids did all the spending. So anytime, Angela asked for money to run the home, he always said: he does not have money. Angela became very frustrated owing to Fiifi's behavior, so she confronted him and it ended up in a big quarrel.

RECIPE
WATERMELON HARD CRUSHES WITH ICE
Ingredients
10 ounces of Endurance
10 ounces of perseverance
10 ounces of patience

METHOD
May the God who gives endurance and encouragement give you a spirit of unity among yourselves as you follow Christ Jesus (Romans 15:5). Sometimes, certain misfortunes or supposed bad things happen to us so that we can know Christ. Angela's frustration should be to know Christ. When Christ comes into the heart it makes us be at peace even though we may be facing storms. Then Jesus said to his disciples, if anyone would come after me, he must deny himself and take up his cross and follow me (Matthew 16:24).

43. THE PROBLEM: THREE IS A CROWD

Dianne and Scott are childhood friends, when Scott got married to Ariel; Dianne was the maid of honor at their wedding. This shows how close Dianne and Scott were. Two years into the marriage, Ariel felt that Dianne and Scott were too close for comfort. So she started monitoring them to find out if they were more than friends. She followed them in taxis anytime they were going out together, till she was caught one day. It destroyed the relationship totally and Scott lost his childhood friend. To Ariel's utter dismay, the two of them were planning Dianne's wedding to a Scottish prince.

RECIPE
WHOLESOME LOVE BREAD AND CORN PORRIDGE
Ingredients
10 ounces of positive thoughts
5 ounces of friendliness
2 ounces of privacy

METHOD
We should never harbor evil thoughts as children of God; a little yeast spoils the whole bread. Rather we should allow ourselves to be used by God for unification purposes and not for divisional purposes. Space is always needed in a relationship, when we love someone we should not hold the person captive, God is love. Now the Lord is the spirit, and where the spirit of the Lord is, there is freedom (1 Corinthians 3:17).

44. THE PROBLEM: THERE IS A BUMP IN THE WAY

Sarah has four children and a great husband. One morning, Sarah got up feeling very tired, she wondered why she couldn't get up. She called in at work and told her manager she was not feeling well so she will come the following day. She hurried off to Dr. Mayfair's clinic and Dr. Mayfair conducted some medical tests on her. She waited in the patio in the hospital reading a local newspaper. A nurse called her name; she quickly put the newspaper down into the newspaper rack and went straight into the doctor's office. Dr. Mayfair had been their family doctor for years and so she was trusted. Dr. Mayfair smiled and said, Sarah you are having a baby. Sarah was stunned; she got home and waited to break the news to her husband. When her husband came in, Sarah told her she was pregnant, she was crying that her life was ruined. Her husband was devastated as well they did not plan for this, they were so unhappy.

RECIPE
RED GRAPE JUICE
Ingredients
10 ounces of embracing grape fruit
10 ounces of love

METHOD
Whichever way you look at it, a child is a gift from God, he chooses to give you that gift and he has a purpose for that child. No child creates a financial burden when we allow God to direct our path. Once he has given you that child he will surely provide for him or her. So relax and sip the red juice. Many are the plans in a man's heart, but it is the Lord's purpose that prevails (Proverbs 19: 21). God knows the end from the beginning, let us trust him fully and rest in the finished work of Christ and yet his works has been finished since the creation of the world (Hebrews 4:3).

45. THE PROBLEM: THE IMPERFECT PAIR

Ada has been married to Kojo for as long as I can remember, Kojo never believed in God and doubted if he ever existed. He was always lying and deceiving people. Ada on the other hand was a Christian who lived her life according to the word of God. Ada thought her husband does not deserve to have her as a wife. So she began to dislike Kojo so much that the sight of him really irritated her. At the end of it all, she wanted a way out because she was tired of the marriage.

RECIPE
PERFECT PEAR COOKIES
Ingredients
10 ounces of love
A pinch of endurance salt
10 ounces of patience

METHOD
Rule of thumb, we cannot fix anyone only God can and God is the only judge of human behavior. Ada cannot fold her arms and judge her husband in ways in which he is not healed. Do not judge and you will not be judged? Do not condemn and you will not be condemned. Forgive and you will be forgiven (Luke 6:37). She should resort to prayer for God to heal her husband and even herself. Most times the hurt that causes us to act most strongly in our partners are almost all the time a reflection of our own. God makes no mistakes in giving us life partners here on earth. Sometimes God brings us together so that we can help each other with God being the head of the marriage. When we exhibit chaste conducts, we set examples for our partners to follow and through Christ their lives changes us well and they are won over (1 Peter 3).

46. THE PROBLEM: CORPORATE AFFAIR

A thick tall man walked into the office and handed some files to Alana to work on and get back to him in an hour's time. That was Samson, Alana's boss. Alana was a married woman with two kids who lived a couple of houses away from where she worked. The truth is Alana's boss was hitting on her and she was torn between her marriage and her career.

RECIPE
RIGHTEOUS RICE PUDDING
Ingredients
10 cups of righteousness
10 cups of love
10 cups of boldness

METHOD
In situations like these, the right thing to do is to ask what the Lord will want you to do. Pray to God for a way out of the situation, God our ever helper will help us in times of need and always keep in mind the golden rule: so in everything, do to others what you would have them do to you, for this sums up the Law and the prophets (Matthew 7:12).

47. THE PROBLEM: THE FAMILY ISSUE

Joe was quarreling with his mum over some family issues. Betty, Joe's wife on the other hand was fueling the estranged relationship between Joe and the mother by branding Joe's mother as a bad woman.

RECIPE
PEACE PIPING ICING
Ingredients
10 ounces of peace
10 ounces of love

METHOD
We are normally unconscious of our own behavior; however we see it in others. When we criticize and make judgements about people we sow a seed of a hate relationship. Blessed are the peacemakers for they shall be called the children of God (Matthew 5: 9). If you are a child of God then you should allow yourself to be used as a vessel to bring peace to people around you. You should be an arbitrator working towards a goal of unity wherever you find yourself.

48. THE PROBLEM: THE NANNY

Ayesha needed a nanny so she could start school, so she called the domestic help agency to find out whether they could get her one. The agency called back in two weeks with a suitable nanny for her. She was so happy and relieved at the same time. Now she could attend classes in peace. After a while, Ayesha started maltreating the nanny and above all her salary was not forthcoming. So her husband complained one day about how she mistreats the nanny and how uncomfortable he was seeing such an attitude coming from no other person but his wife. He continued that he feels so ashamed anytime he doesn't pay her and he doesn't have money to pay the nanny too. Ayesha got offended and snapped back, she is my nanny not yours, you are invading my space!

RECIPE
REWARDING FRENCH FRIES AND SIZZLING SAUSAGES
Ingredients
10 ounces of love
10 ounces of Christ
10 ounces of letting go

METHOD
Look! The wages you failed to pay the workmen who mowed your fields are crying out against you. The cries of the harvesters have reached the ears of the Lord Almighty! (James 5:4). As a Christian, you are supposed to live the life that Christ lived, setting your minds on things above not on earthly desires (Colossians 3).

49. THE PROBLEM: THE CHILDLESS COUPLE

A couple has been childless for ten years. The issue has made the wife very saucy and very disrespectful at home. Their situation is making them so unhappy.

RECIPE
GIFT SNACK CAKE (DESSERT)
Ingredients
5 ounces of patience flour
5 ounces of prayer
5 ounces of rest

METHOD
Note: A dessert is served after the main meal. Children are the desserts in a marriage. Children are a gift from God; it is God who gives not man. Sons are a heritage from the Lord, children a reward from him (Psalm 127:3). The focus on the marriage should be on the love that the couple share, and if God decides to reward the couple with children, fine. Children should not be the main reason why people should marry; marriage is to give companionship and love to each other. However, the couple can also ask God for children in prayer and wait patiently for God's answer in his own time.

50. THE PROBLEM: THE BURNT STEW

Juju worked tirelessly taking care of three kids and cooking at the same time on weekends. She managed to prepare chicken stew for the family to accompany the left over rice in the rice cooker for lunch. The husband came home after volley ball practice and put the chicken stew on fire and slept off. When Juju got down from the bedroom upstairs, she saw smoke coming out of the kitchen door and she went in hurriedly to find out that her chicken stew was totally burnt. She stormed into the hall where her husband was sleeping and said "You are so irresponsible" I hate you.

RECIPE
MINT CARAMEL
Ingredients
4 ounces of patience
4 ounces of love
4 ounces of mint

METHOD
It is very annoying to realize the stew you put so much effort in has been burnt, but we need to be patient with everyone bearing with each other. However, you can get angry for a moment, but in your anger do not say certain words that you may regret later. "Hate is a harsh word to use for anybody, let alone someone you love. Do not let any unwholesome talk come out from your mouths, but only what is helpful for building others up according to their needs, that it may benefit those who listen (Ephesians 4:29).

51. THE PROBLEM: BATHING TIME

Serwaa had done the laundry, the previous day and was folding the clothes in the living room whilst her husband was busy chit chatting on his phone. The couple shared a five year old son who wanted to have a bath. Mummy said Cree; I want to have a bath. Mummy told Cree, tell daddy to give you a bath, he is less busy than I am. Daddy overheard their conversation and said hey I am bathing no one, I am very tired.

RECIPE
PATIENCE CREAM PUDDING
Ingredient
4 ounces of communicators
4 ounces of patience flour
A teaspoon of sugar spice

METHOD
Rule of thumb in marriage is not to look at your partner's behavior or actions but seek unconditional love through Christ. Men generally have a bossy attitude, however as Christians we must clothe ourselves with compassion, kindness, humility, gentleness and patience (Colossians 3:12). Communicating with your husband at another time about him helping you when needed will be very necessary. Moreover, when we bear the fruits of the spirit, we tend to focus more on what the word of God says and not react based on actions or inactions of people, for the spirit gives life and the flesh kills.

52. THE PROBLEM: THE HUGE ROCK

Honey I think I deserve that giant diamond ring we saw at the jewelry shop yesterday, for my hard work in this marriage said Mrs. Extravagant. Mr. Extravagant then looked back at his wife of five years and wondered why such a "silly" demand when he was even trying to pay the house rent. I am sorry but I do not think I can afford it, Mr. Extravagant simply replied. Mrs. Extravagant concluded what a shame! You cannot even get your wife, a ring she so deserves.

RECIPE
FORGET -ME –OUGHT
Ingredients
1 cup of love
1 cup of understanding
1 cup of contentment

METHOD
Rings are symbols worn to signify that one is married; however, rings do not define a marriage. The type of ring worn does not really matter what really matters is the love that both of you share. Love is reasonable and not forceful or compelling. As Christians, we need to be content with whatever we have and be appreciative of the situation in which we are in. At the right time, if Mr. Extravagant can buy that huge diamond ring for his wife, that is fine.

53. THE PROBLEM: THE UNWORKING HUSBAND

Nhyira's husband lost her job after ten years of working in the hospital due to misconduct. Nhyira was taking care of a family of five singlehandedly. She begun to mistreat her husband and making him do things he could not afford. Nhyira's husband had to resort to borrowing to keep up with his wife outrageous demands, and then her husband got fed up and left the house.

RECIPE
SWEET PEA SOUP
Ingredients
1 cup of love
1 cup of patience
1 cup of submission

METHOD
As wives, we are supposed to be the emotional support for our husbands. Love is patient, comforting and submissive. This is the time when Nhyira's husband needs the wife the most, he has lost his job. As such, we should be the comfort he needs not the other way round so that he can get up on his feet. Praise be to the God and father of our Lord Jesus Christ, the father of compassion and the God of all comfort who comforts us in our troubles, so that we can comfort those in any trouble with the comfort we ourselves have received from God (2 Corinthians 1:3-4). As a Christian, we need to encourage others in the Lord just as Christ encourages and strengthens us when we are in need.

54. THE PROBLEM: THE TURNED TABLES

Mr. Bad had a very lucrative job, a great family and a good social life, let's conclude that Mr. Bad had it all. He was the envy of all his friends, everybody thought Mr. Bad was a lucky man and of course he was. It was like he had the Midas touch, everything he touched turned into gold. Meanwhile, his wife Mrs. Bad was so unhappy in the marriage, she was being mistreated by her husband because she was financially dependent on him. Mrs. Bad prayed to God and God heard her plea. Mrs. Bad gained admission to study law with full scholarship plus stipend every month. Mrs. Bad was overjoyed, she begun studying without worrying about her fees or where her next meal will come from. God had provided it all. After four years Mrs. Bad had completed her law degree and went further to school to be called to the bar. Mrs. Bad was now a qualified lawyer and she got employed by a high profile law firm. Her salary was four times that of her husband's salary. Mrs. Bad helped Mr. Bad by taking care of the home financially. Mr. Bad was so ashamed; he wished he had treated his wife better when he had the chance to do so.

RECIPE
CHICKEN CHANGE SALAD
Ingredients
1 cup of love
1 cup of tolerance
1 cup of humility

METHOD
The fact in life is that no condition is permanent and change is the constant thing in life. It is not what happens to you that matters, but it is how you react to it that counts. When our thoughts are clean it reflects our actions no matter the situation. The best revenge is not rubbing successes in people's faces and being proud about it. It is through grace, you have been successful, so no one should boast. Therefore people should be treated in the most

compassionate and forgiving way. Do not be overcome by evil, but overcome evil with good (Romans 12:21).

55. THE PROBLEM: KEEPING UP WITH THE AFFLUENTS

Eva and Adam were a married couple for as far as I could remember. They lived in a decent house across the street and operated a family business. The house next to them became vacant and a new neighbor, Mr. and Mrs. Affluent moved in with their children. Mr. and Mrs. Affluent had moved from the big city to the suburbs. Eva admired the rich life of the Affluent's and wished same for herself. She begun to peep at them through the window, she saw them holding hands and laughing. Oh gosh! Their living room was so gorgeous! Eva started worrying her husband to give her such a life. Her husband could not understand why such a behavior. Gradually, they were heading towards split Ville.

RECIPE
COMPARE- ME KNOTS
Ingredients
1 cup of love
1 cup of contentment
1 cup of focus cream

METHOD
You want something but don't get it. You kill and covet, but you cannot have what you want. You quarrel and fight. You do not have because you do not ask God (James 4:2). Rule of thumb, never compare yourself with others because you do not know anything about the person's situation and do not know the skeletons in his or her cupboard. It is good to admire other people's marriages but when your neighbor's marriage is making you feel less secured about yours, then there is a problem. Also you can take a selfie, by examining yourself first to find out how you can change to make your marriage better than the way it is. Focus on Christ and channel all your

frustrations into prayer for God's will to be done for you in his perfect time.

56. THE PROBLEM: I HAVE BEEN TURNED INTO A BABY MAKING MACHINE

Kofi and Mila have been married for twelve years. Kofi is a banker and Mila is a stay at home mom. Mila is a stay at home mom due to circumstances beyond her control; she is always popping babies out every two years. Mila had a conversation with her husband Kofi, this is not the life I bargained for, I want more than this, she complained. Kofi as usual did not say a word. Mila was left sitting in her rocking chair, she said sadly to herself he has the career and I have just nothing.

RECIPE
CORN STIRR PUDDING
Ingredients
1 ounce of patience
1 ounce of contentment
1 ounce of love

METHOD
In as much as gender roles have changed over time, women are still the primary care givers of children. However as married couples, we are supposed to complement each other so that each one can achieve his or her dream individually. Some misfortunes can be disguised blessings. If Mila can turn her face to the wall and pray with the contrite spirit that God desires, God can make it possible for her to have a career and take care of her children at the same time with none suffering. At times, the person we get married to normally teaches us more about ourselves than we ever know. I call them pushers, they will push you to the extent that God will be your all dependency and he will provide what you need at that particular time and even beyond.

57. THE PROBLEM: THE GAME CHANGER

Sharon's husband is ten years older than she is. Sharon is young and beautiful and full of life whilst her husband is nearing retirement and is not enthusiastic about life anymore. Anytime, Sharon discusses any plans with her husband, her husband throws it all away. Sharon was getting frustrated and was contemplating divorce.

RECIPE
LOOK AWAY SOUP WITH BREAD
Ingredients
10 cups of close relationship with God
10 cups of love

METHOD
There is good in everything, if only we take our time to look for it. Maybe, Sharon's husband is telling her, I am not your guide, God is! This is the fact. When we build an interpersonal relationship with God, we acknowledge him in everything we do and he directs our path. Sharon might be the game changer who could lead the family to success and the husband tagging along through Christ.

58. THE PROBLEM: WORRY NOT!

Mrs. A is angry that her husband has not paid the children's school fees and the reopening day is approaching. Mr. A on the other hand has some challenges in paying the fees which Mrs. A does not understand so she is filing for divorce.

RECIPE
FREE PANCAKES
Ingredients
1 cup of reasoning
1 cup of love
1 cup of patience

METHOD
Love is when we are reasonable with each other. Mrs. A should resort to prayer so that the peace of God will guard her heart. God will definitely send help on the way at the right time. May be the help will even come through her. Therefore do not worry about tomorrow, for tomorrow will worry about itself. Each day has enough troubles of its own (Matthew 6:34).

59. THE PROBLEM: THE PRAYER WARRIOR

Mrs. Amen frequents prayer meetings to the disgust of her husband. She is never at home; the church is basically her home. One fateful day, Mrs. Amen quickly dashed out of their home and hurriedly closed the main door after her. She was heading to church for a prayer meeting. Her husband said: Mrs. Amen, you just returned home and there is absolutely nothing at home for the kids and me to eat, could you please sort us out before you go. Mrs. Amen replied: I have to go and pray to God, I am running late. Mr. Amen could not take it any longer and he is seeking for a divorce.

RECIPE
EVER THERE MARSHMALLOWS
Ingredients
A dash of love
A sprinkle of timely flour
Ever there toppings

METHOD
God gives us families on earth so that we can support their needs and wants through him. As a Christian, your family is your first ministry and you need to be responsible for their upkeep through Christ who gives you strength. As a wife, serving your husband is serving Christ. God is an omnipresent God, what makes you think God will not listen to your prayer if you pray at home whilst taking care of your family. Prayer meetings are not bad, but let us focus more on building an interpersonal relationship with Christ for the Holy Spirit to guide us in our lives for the prayer of the righteous is powerful and effective (James 5:16).

60. THE PROBLEM: THE SEX CONTRACT

Anna feels her husband demands too much sex and she is tired. She wants a sex contract to be signed where they will have sex twice a week. Joey, Anna's husband always wants to be intimate with his wife and feels devastated at such a sex contract.

RECIPE
CONSENSUS PIE
A cup of communication
A cup of prioritizers
A cup of love

METHOD
Being intimate with your partner is what spices a good marriage. When you marry, you become one flesh. So see it as anything you do to a partner you are doing it to yourself and put yourself in each other's shoes and see how both of you will feel. The first step is communication with each other to find out why they are at extreme ends when it comes to being intimate with each other. Perhaps the communication will unleash hidden problems that both have refused to talk about so that they can get to a favorable decision. The wife does not have authority over her own body but yields it to her husband. In the same way, the husband does not have authority over his own body but yields it to his wife. (1 Corinthians 7:4)

61. THE PROBLEM: OUR BEDROOM IS MINE

Mary complained bitterly to her best friend Lilian, My husband never sleeps in the bedroom with me. He always falls asleep whilst watching television late in the night. I am always alone. I am really in pain and anytime I try to have that conversation with him, he dismisses my query and reacts negatively to it. He does not know the extent to which this situation is affecting me.

RECIPE
ASANA WITH LOVE CUBES
Ingredients
2 packets of love cubes
4 ounces of communication flour
A dash of patient toppings
A bucketful of prayer

METHOD
You cannot control your partner's behavior, so don't attack directly. Send all your frustration to God through prayer. After prayer, allow time and have that conversation again with the guidance of the Holy Spirit. When you and your partner are heading towards different directions other than reaching a consensus through decision making, know that it is not you or them but it is an opportunity to know God and grow maturing in God's love. As Christians, we are supposed to rise above the situation through God who strengthens us and not be submerged by any situation. Furthermore, that he would grant you, according to the riches of his glory, to be strengthened with might by his spirit in the inner man (Ephesians 3:16).

62. THE PROBLEM: THE TROPHY WIFE

Mrs. Addo was being treated like a trophy wife; her husband dotes on her to the extent that the treatment is beginning to irritate her. She just wants to be normal.

RECIPE
ENJOY SUNDAES
Ingredients
2 cups of appreciation
2 cups of communication
2 cups of patience
2 cups of tolerance

METHOD
Okay, let's get it here, every girl or woman wants to be treated as a queen. Most women would really want to be in Mrs. Addo's shoes. However, every woman is different and wishes to be treated in a particular way. Space is one of the most important things in everybody's life. The space to be independent and to think or take decisions on your own is most of the time necessary. However, Mrs. Addo can have a frank communication with her husband as to why she doesn't want to be doted on; perhaps her husband will understand and give her the necessary space that she needs. With patience and tolerance and love Mrs. Addo can get what she wants without hurting the partner's feelings.

63. THE PROBLEM: THE VALENTNE'S DAY SET BACK

Akua has been so crazy about Valentine's Day ever since she fell in love with her now hubby Paul. Every valentine's day, Akua receives a bouquet of flowers from Paul and she will be so happy and feel loved. The day before Valentine's Day that year, Paul was in a series of meeting at work as they were planning the budget for financial analysis. The next day, Akua was so full of excitement as she waited for her bouquet of flowers. She waited and waited, there was no sign of any bouquet of flowers. In short, Paul had forgotten all about Valentine's Day because he had not really recovered from the previous day exhaustion at work. Akua was very disappointed in Paul and in the marriage as well.

RECIPE
MILD SHITO SAUCE
Ingredients
10 ounces of love
2 cups of communication
1 cup of letting go

METHOD
Marriage is exhibiting unconditional love to your respective spouses at all times. When love turns into hate, we attack our partner's behavior. Love is whole and as such we need to love the whole being as it is, not what he or she fails or fail not to do. When Akua is able to communicate with him, she will find out the reason why he forgot to get her the bouquet of flowers on Valentine's Day. Live everyday as Valentine's Day and learn to live above your partner's mistakes or forgetfulness. May the God who gives endurance and encouragement give you the same attitude of mind toward each other that Christ Jesus had, so that with one mind and one voice you may glorify the God and Father of our Lord Jesus Christ (Romans 15:5-6).

64. THE PROBLEM: THE WRESTLERS

Edna and Ike are constantly fighting for as long as I can remember. Edna feels Ike is not a good husband and never stays at home to take care of the kids they have together as a couple. At the least chance possible, they enter the wrestling ring and quarrel like nobody's business.

RECIPE
PEACE SMOKED FISH STEW
Ingredients
1 cup of prayer
2 cups of love
A ¼ of peace smoked fish

METHOD
Marriage is not a battlefield, when situations happen, on the spot we want to respond, but we should refrain from responding automatically when we are pissed off. We should transfer all our automatic responses into prayer for our struggle is not against flesh and blood, but against the rulers, against the authorities, against the powers of this dark world and against the spiritual forces of evil in the heavenly realms. Therefore put on the full armor of God, so that when the day of evil comes, you may be able to stand your ground, and after you have done everything, to stand, stand firm (Ephesians 6:12-13). The solution is not fighting with each other, we are fighting a common enemy and we can overcome the enemy through prayer and living according to the word of God.

65. THE PROBLEM: "THE BOMBSHELL"

Jenny received a word of knowledge that her husband was not the man she should have married and that she should leave her husband to pave the way for God's divine choice. Jenny went home and started misbehaving, because she wanted a way out. Jenny's husband Nii was a kind hearted man who loved God and there were no problems in the marriage until now. Nii didn't know what had come over his wife, so he had a conversation with jenny to find out what the problem was. Jenny spilled the beans that a supposed man of God has told her that he wasn't the right man for her, so she wants out. Nii was dumbfounded, how can it be? I prayed and God chose you for me he said sadly.

RECIPE
PRAYER SOUP
Ingredients
5 ounces of prayer
5 ounces of love
5 ounces of discernment
5 ounces of patience

METHOD
Jenny should not be in haste to make decisions based on the word of knowledge received. Jenny should pray to be able to discern whether the word of knowledge is really from God. Dear friends, do not believe every spirit, but test the spirits to see whether they are from God, because many false prophets have gone out into the world (1 John 4:1).

66. THE PROBLEM: THE TALE THAT WASN'T

Amal left home hurriedly to the Martins grocery store. She has been a sales girl for two years in Martins, the largest grocery store in the suburb. Her husband, Job, was a mechanic at George's garage, the oldest mechanic shop in the suburb where they lived. Word got to Job that Amal was flirting around. Job was a thick tall man and he was feared in the neighborhood because of his size. He confronted Amal on the issue and Amal denied it vehemently although it was true. Job thought there was a little truth in the rumor so he therefore decided to watch his wife carefully. Lo and behold, he caught them red-handed. Job was shattered but because he loved his wife, he decided to give her another chance. However, Amal feels ashamed and wants out of the marriage.

RECIPE
HONESTY BEEF LOAVES
Ingredients
6 ounces of love
A sprinkle of humility
A dash of Appreciation

METHOD
Sometimes the initial spark in the marriage is gone due to other responsibilities. It is our duty however to bring that spark back, by letting God into our lives. Temptations always happen even as God's children but no temptation has overtaken you except what is common to mankind. And God is faithful; he will not let you be tempted beyond what you can bear. But when you are tempted, he will also provide a way out so that you can endure it (1 Corinthians 10:13). We all make mistakes all the time, as such if you have failed at some point, acknowledge the mistake, learn to say I am sorry and move on. It is also so relieving to find out that the other partner has already forgiven you and he or she is willing to live above that mistake and allow God to take control. So therefore, embrace the present, forget about the past and move on.

67. THE PROBLEM: THE UNSATISFIED WOMAN

Mr. and Mrs. Joy have been married for ten years with twin girls. Mr. Joy has been recently diagnosed with cancer and is also suffering with erectile dysfunction. Mrs. Joy wants out of the marriage because Mr. Joy cannot satisfy her sexually as he used to.

RECIPE
CHANGE GROUNDNUT GARI SOAKINGS
Ingredients
4 ounces of love
2 ounces of patience
1 ounce of prayer

METHOD
Mr. and Mrs. Joy have always enjoyed an active sex life until now, which is actually no fault of Mr. Joy. This is the time that Mr. Joy needs his wife the most. Sex is an ingredient that spices our marriage but since it is because of a health reason that Mrs. Joy is not being satisfied. Mrs. Joy should pray about it and God will fill that vacuum in her life for her to endure until God's time when he decides to bring a solution to the problem. It is valuable to lose something that you really wanted or enjoyed, because it is in that loss, that we are encouraged to build ourselves in Christ.

68. THE PROBLEM: THE CAR

Mark has been married to May for two years and they were still in the process of knowing each other. May worked in a construction firm so she owned a pick-up truck whilst Mark had a salon car. Mark's best friend Peter was moving out of his house and hence needed a pick up car to convey some of his stuff to his new apartment. One weekend, Mark gave Peter the car without consulting his wife. His wife got to know about it and she was done with the marriage.

RECIPE
KINDNESS MILK SHAKE
Ingredients
10 ounces love
4 ounces of kindness
A cup of letting go

METHOD
Every time stuff happens, it is not what happens to you, but how you react to it which can either be positive or negative. Sometimes, the other partner in a relationship will push you to develop certain attributes which will be helpful to you this time or later. The way and manner in which Mark gave the car to Peter was not right, however kindness overrides being right in a situation. May, on the other hand should learn to forgive Mark and let God take control of her life. God is kind and God is love.

69. THE PROBLEM: UNDEFINED BRAND

Mrs. Bitter disrespects and maltreats Mr. Bitter at home, for reasons best known to her. She even goes to the extent of shouting at him when neighbors are around. This behavior makes Mr. Bitter very uncomfortable around Mrs. Bitter. He feels Mrs. Bitter does not regard him as a husband, let alone respect him and he feels so useless. He then met a lady who treated him so nicely ever. Gradually, the king in him was being revealed. He consequently separated from his wife and the wife realized that she wants her husband back.

RECIPE
BRANDED APPLE SAUCE
Ingredients
½ cup respect
½ cup submission
½ cup royal aroma
½ cup branding

METHOD
Wives submit to your husbands, as is fitting in the Lord (Colossians 3:18). If you claim you love God, you need to submit to your husband unconditionally. Not taking into consideration his current situation or resources, submit, that is all, which comes out of mutual love for each other. When we are able to live according to Christ's teaching, we have a sweet fragrance that cannot be ignored by all. We should also try and define our brand, by holding on dearly to what God has given to us and nurturing it according to the principles of Christ. And whatever you do, whether in word or deed, do it all in the name of the Lord Jesus, giving thanks to God the Father through him (Colossians 3:17).

70. THE PROBLEM: THE INSENSITIVE MAN

Mr. and Mrs. Adams were married for ten years. They started drifting apart because of financial issues. Mrs. Adams on one of her busy schedules was driving the kids to school when she accidentally hit another oncoming car. It was such a scene. Mrs. Adams was already disorganized and now she was confused. She therefore called her husband Mr. Adams who was at work. Mr. Adam a workaholic on the other hand was married to his work and as such did not want any disturbances from home during working hours. When Mrs. Adams name showed as the caller ID on his phone, he wondered why she was calling him at such a time. He thought to himself, I am not going back home if there was any problem, I have so much to do at work. He picked the phone reluctantly and Mrs. Adam said hello at the other end of the phone, he answered back grumpily; hello what is it? Mrs. Adams told him I am involved in a little accident down Mesa Street; could you come and help me please? So is this why you called, I am busy at work! Mr. Adam did not ask if she was hurt, whether the kids were okay, or anything else concerning their well-being. Mrs. Adams was so devastated and hanged up.

RECIPE
BANANA SKY (Turn to the sky and seek the face of Christ)
Ingredients
½ cup of patience
¼ cup of love
¼ cup of prayer

METHOD
First thing is for Mrs. Adams to pray to God for guidance and direction in such a situation and God will give her the peace that cannot be understood by human minds (Philippians 4). Prayer puts you at rest knowing that God is in control of the situation; therefore turning to God first is the way to go. I lift up my eyes to the hills, where does my help comes from? My help comes from the Lord, the maker of heaven and earth (Psalm 121:1-2). Yes the

husband has been so insensitive, not asking anything concerning their well-being, but love should be unconditional, you should be able to love your husband not based on what he does or does not do. Unfortunately or fortunately, sometimes the Christian wife has to live an exemplary life as Christ did to win her husband over with her chaste conduct (1 Peter 3). Love is also patient, just as Christ has been so patient with us from the beginning we also ought to be patient with each other. When, Mrs. Adams makes a banana sky out of patience, love and prayer. God will walk her through the problem and she will be at peace. God may even send the appropriate help that she needs, for he only searches our hearts and knows our minds and knows exactly what we need.

May the grace of the Lord Jesus Christ, and the love of God, and the fellowship of the Holy Spirit be with you all (2 Corinthians 13:14).

The Marriage Cook Book

Adwoba Addo-Boateng

www.ingramcontent.com/pod-product-compliance
Lightning Source LLC
Chambersburg PA
CBHW052200110526
44591CB00012B/2026